THE GARDEN PATH

THE LIBRARY *of* GARDEN DETAIL

THE GARDEN
PATH

PATRICK TAYLOR

Simon and Schuster
New York   London   Toronto   Sydney   Tokyo   Singapore

Simon and Schuster

Simon & Schuster Building

Rockefeller Center

1230 Avenue of the Americas

New York, New York 10020

Text Copyright © 1991 by Patrick Taylor

Photographic credits listing on page 63

First published in Great Britain in 1991 by
Pavilion Books Limited

196 Shaftesbury Avenue, London WC2H 8JL

Designed by Paul Burcher

Printed and bound in Italy by L.E.G.O., Vicenza

Library of Congress Cataloguing in Publication Data

Taylor, Patrick.
    The garden path/Patrick Taylor.
        p. cm.—(The Library of garden detail)
    "First published in Great Britain in 1991 by Pavilion Books
Limited"—T.p. verso.
    ISBN 0-671-74402-X (cloth)
    1. Garden walks—Design and construction. I. Title. II. Series.
TH4970.T39 1991
717—dc20

                                            91-8760
                                              CIP

10   9   8   7   6   5   4   3   2   1

CONTENTS

✦

INTRODUCTION
page 7

GRASS
page 27

STONE
page 36

WOOD
page 49

BRICK
page 54

SOURCES
page 62

CREDITS
page 63

6

INTRODUCTION

ATHS LEAD THE EYE, OR THE FOOTSTEP, INTO THE GARDEN picture and provide the single most valuable ingredient of garden design. Few images are so desolate as the notion of a land without paths, a trackless waste. One of the oldest communities in Britain – the lake-village people of Somerset – made the earliest known surfaced path in the world in about 4000 BC, the Sweet Track to Glastonbury, miraculously preserved to this day in the peat. In England, ancient landscape is often patterned with 'holloways', those primeval roads, typically edged with trees and mossy banks, that seem to be worn deeply into the ground by the passage of countless feet and hooves. Paths are of primarily functional purpose but they are also a vivid sign of wilderness tamed, of order introduced into chaos. In gardens this orderliness gives a purposeful structure.

7

To lead someone up the garden path – meaning to deceive – is a relatively modern expression, dating from the 1920s. Before that it had the more attractive sense of gently persuasive courtship. This underlines one of the most important functions of the path – the power to lure the visitor on to other delights. A well-planned path serves many purposes in the garden apart from the merely practical one of providing a durable and dry surface between two points. As an ingredient of garden design the path has versatility, sublety and vitality.

8

Most gardens are immediately adjacent to houses and here paths may provide an essential visual link between house and garden – extending the architecture into the greenery. In the case of traditional houses this means that paths will inevitably be straight and laid out in a rectilinear plan. The bias in favour of straight paths is an old one. William Lawson in *A New Orchard and Garden* (1618) wrote 'universallie walks are straight'. J. C. Loudon in his great *Encyclopaedia of Gardening* (1822) regards the matter as one of

Holy Writ, certainly handed down on tablets of stone, and conceivably received direct from the Almighty: 'The principle of *a sufficient reason* should never be lost sight of in laying out walks . . . that is, no deviation from a straight line should ever appear, for which a reason is not given in the

1. *The archetypal cottage front-garden with a concrete path that runs straight from the entrance gate to the front door.*

9

position of the ground, trees, or other accompanying objects.' This certainly represents the western ideal of path-making and even in the landscape, woodland or meadow garden paths should not wind in an arbitrary way.

As William Gilpin wrote of the approach drive to a house in his *Remarks on Forest Scenery* (1791), 'Let it wind: but let it not take any deviation which is not well accounted for.' Thomas Jefferson, deeply immersed in eighteenth-century garden ideas, in his garden at Monticello designed the paths to follow the contours of his hillside.

In China, however, things were very different. The influential gardening manual *Yuan Yeh* (1634) recommends that 'the paths meander like playing cats' and such sinuous lines are certainly more harmonious with the asymmetry and aesthetic playfulness of Chinese gardens. A curved path also implies a more leisurely walk, encouraging the visitor to pause, reflect and admire – an essential part of the contemplative nature of Eastern gardens.

There is in Chinese and Japanese gardens an entire aesthetic of garden paths in which the surface materials, the disposition of the parts and the way fallen leaves lie upon them, are essential qualities. Here is Jiro Harada's description of the principles of path-making in a *cha-no-yu* garden –

a type of garden which aims to make beautiful the mundane objects of everyday life: 'Any apparent regularity should be avoided, as the beauty of the stepping-stones is best obtained by studied irregularity ... The order of the sequence in placing differently shaped stones needs study and practice. The indented part of the one should be supplemented by pointing towards it the projection of the next ... The distance between the stones should be somewhat varied, but approximately five or six inches (8 to 10 cm) are allowed, and they should be about two to five inches (3.5 to 8 cm) exposed above the ground ... The height takes into consideration the growth of moss on the ground and also pine needles with which the ground is covered in order to protect the moss or the ground against frost.'

2. *A naturalistic effect is beautifully achieved in this path of stepping stones.*

11

In European gardens there is a sternly utilitarian view of paths. Art may well enter into their making but their first purpose is practical. They should have a point – they must go somewhere, as directly as possible. 'They should not,' wrote Russell Page, 'be made where they are not necessary . . . I know of nothing that makes a garden more forlorn than an unused path.' Paths with a purpose, that carry out their function as economically as possible, certainly have a calm reasonableness about them, and a well-conceived pattern of paths may give the essential framework to a garden design. On the other hand, a path curving out of sight or one whose goal is not at first apparent, can give an attractive air of mystery and surprise.

The width of a garden path is something that is worth thinking about carefully. The classic rule is that any path should be wide enough to allow two people to saunter easily side by side. That is fine for those who like to lead their lives by classic rules – which are often no more than an excuse for not thinking about the matter. J. C. Loudon, characteristically, goes into things more deeply. He says that no path should be narrower than four feet six inches (1.5m) but he also points out that for, say, two dozen people to walk abreast – 'thirty-six feet suffices'. That sort of thing

3. *In this plantsman's garden a very narrow serpentine path of stone flags winds its way through mixed borders boldly edged with hostas. Such narrow paths suit informal planting and allow close viewing of plants.*

will not be a burning problem in many gardens today but the width of paths in general in relation to their context and their use must be considered carefully. A very narrow path, allowing the passage of one person only, mysteriously

14

4. *In this formal garden different surface materials are mixed to brilliant
effect. The path of old bricks, laid with repeated circles that give a
foretaste of the rondel of clipped hornbeam* (Carpinus betulus) *beyond,
leads down to a finely-laid path of square stone slabs.*

penetrating some profusely planted area, can be very enticing. At East Lambrook Manor Margery Fish deployed her paths to suit perfectly the romanticized cottage garden she made there. For most of her paths she used irregular pieces of the local limestone and they scarcely ever follow a straight line. Very narrow paths, sometimes merely stepping stones, thread their way through the dense planting bringing the visitor close to the plants. As many of these are rare, or carefully chosen forms of wild plants, it is part of the purpose of the garden to, as it were, rub the visitor's nose in them. Seeds sow themselves between the stones and good plants are allowed to remain, both ornamenting the path and giving an atmosphere of impermanence, of nature fighting back to reclaim her territory. This is completely different from, say, the intentions of Beatrix Farrand in the great garden at Dumbarton Oaks. Here, the paths are an integral part of a grand formal conception; their materials are fastidiously chosen to harmonize with the architectural setting.

15

A path that is too wide for its setting, on the other hand, can, like too much soda in the whisky, dilute the effect to insipidness. In general terms a path between borders of equal width should be no wider than half the width of each border. A central path between two lavishly planted borders provides both a visual breathing space and access to admire their beauty. It should not draw attention to itself by being ostentatiously large or made of an obtrusive material.

There are many materials from which paths may be made. Some – such as York paving, a fine-textured lime-stone – seem to look well in almost any garden setting. York paving with its unassertive pale grey colour and slightly irregular surface gives even a newly laid path an air of antiquity. However, a good general rule is that paths near the house should be made of similar material to the house. In East Anglia where houses are generally of brick, paths of the same material, or clay paving slabs, are by far the best surfaces. In old houses and gardens there was, for want of

something worse, a harmony in the very materials used;
now, with mass production and cheap transport, all possible
materials are available all over the country and hideously
discordant effects can be effortlessly achieved. The gardens

5. *An old path of York paving, cracked and
uneven, has great character and associates well
with borders packed with delicate flowers.*

17

designed by Sir Edwin Lutyens and Miss Gertrude Jekyll
showed exceptional sensitivity to appropriate building
materials. At Hestercombe in Somerset, for example, the
paths and walls are made of riven stone quarried on the site,
and stone from nearby Ham Hill is used for all dressed stone

work. This, in a garden exposed to the surrounding countryside, gives colours and textures that harmonize easily with the setting. At Hestercombe the paving stones are of slightly roughly cut irregular rectangles which give an appropriately rustic formality. Finely jointed regular ashlar (hewn stone with straight edges) – admirable for town courtyards – in the country creates an unsympathetically manicured impression. At the other extreme, crazy paving – random shapes of broken paving material – seems one of the most difficult path surfaces to use effectively. At Mount Stewart – a supremely idiosyncratic garden, not made for people who dislike seeing rules successfully broken – Lady Londonderry used it with aristocratic panache. However, in most small gardens, where crazy paving is most frequently seen, such paths create a visual jangle, obtrusively eyecatching and restless. No doubt in some post-modernist gardens that is exactly the effect that is wanted. Cobblestones or setts, although very beautiful to look at, do not make a surface that is very agreeable to walk on. There is no

18

reason to disdain composition, or concrete paving slabs, which are often cast to resemble stone, though I do not care for the slightly undulating bogus York stone effect; I find myself endlessly searching for the repeated pattern. Plain slabs vary considerably in colour, shape and texture but beware of very smooth surfaces which can be dangerously slippery when wet. They also do not acquire so easily the attractive weathered patina which rougher surfaces quickly develop. Clever interlocking shapes, in unlikely colours of oxblood or pale blue, are perfect if you want your garden to resemble a Continental pedestrianized shopping street.

6. This central path made of a row of cement slabs shows attractive variations in colour.

19

To many garden visitors the soothing crunch of gravel and the scent of sun-warmed box hedges are characteristically pleasurable parts of the experience. Gravel makes wonderful paths but the material

needs choosing with care. The wrong kind may not merely
be inappropriate for its setting but can be positively painful
to look at. For example, a large expanse of excessively pale
stone chippings reflects the light too well and creates a
baleful glare on even an overcast day; the bilious yellow of
some lime-stone chippings casts an unpleasantly sickly glow;
equally, chippings of an excessively sombre grey can lend an
air of gloom to the most cheerful of borders. In parts of the
country where local stone is widely used as a building
material it is often possible to acquire chippings from a
nearby quarry which blend harmoniously with buildings and
landscape. True gravel – fine pebbles collected from the
sea-shore or river beds – not only provides a superb surface
but generally has a marvellously attractive subtly speckled
colour.

Grass paths look best either in conjunction with
borders or other closely planted areas, or at some distance
from the house where, perhaps becoming increasingly
roughly mown, they can make an effective transition

7. A path of fine gravel is broken occasionally by
pieces of glistening natural stone. This oriental
effect admirably suits the plantings of azaleas and
Japanese maples (Acer japonicum *species).*

between garden and nature. Beyond the garden, in a
meadow or orchard, a winding close-mown path through
tall grass can have great beauty, and a straight one can
continue a garden vista into the countryside. Formal grass
paths demand much upkeep and will not withstand

intensive use, particularly when they are wet. Plants spilling over from a border on to a grass path can, especially where the edges are kept crisply trimmed, look very attractive but they may soon overshadow and kill the grass. A good

8. *The refined use of harmonious materials distinguishes this inventive formal garden. The path is of brick laid on its edge in an elegant herring-bone pattern and finished with strips of stone on each side.*

solution is to make an edging to the path of brick or stone.

Brick is an immensely versatile surface. At gardens such as Hatfield House in Hertfordshire the beautiful Tudor brick of the house and many of its garden walls and

22

outhouses is echoed in the use of old bricks in the paths. In an elaborate and richly planted garden, this gives a restful harmony. The colour and texture of brick vary tremendously and need to be chosen with care. New brick can look rather startling but it usually weathers satisfactorily. In the London area the attractive slightly yellow-brown tinge of London stock makes an excellent garden path. Bricks may be laid in many different patterns to create a lively surface – basket-weave, herring-bone or different bonds echoing the structure of garden walls or buildings. Laying them on their edge is very uneconomical but a finely laid herring-bone pattern of edge-laid bricks, as is often seen in old gardens in East Anglia, makes a beautiful and elegant path. In George Washington's garden at Mount Vernon the garden walls and buildings are made of brick and paths of square terracotta paviours go well with them.

Wood is a versatile but generally not long-lived path material. In Japanese gardens lengths of bamboo are laid crosswise to form a visually exciting pattern but one that is

23

not very comfortable to walk on. Paths made of decking, planed timber laid in parallel slats with narrow gaps, are practical and make a sympathetic setting for contemporary architecture. Thin cross sections of the trunks of trees, preserving slight irregularities in contour, provide attractive 'stepping stones' in informal parts of a garden. In damp places moss grows well on them and in woodland gardens they blend easily with their surroundings.

A mixture of materials – bricks, stone or gravel alternating in repeated patterns – can make a lively path. The result can sometimes be *too* ornamental, distracting the viewer from the beauty of nearby planting, but such effects go well with an austerely formal planting of clipped hedges and simple topiary.

Some paths – especially of gravel or sand – will need edging to contain the material. In the nineteenth century edging tiles were mass produced to meet the need of expanding numbers of suburban gardens. They were of ceramic, sometimes of a natural terracotta colour and

24

*9. A path of warm-coloured chippings kept firmly
in place by low hedges of box (Buxus
sempervirens). A curved path works well
between informal beds in this woodland setting.*

sometimes a rather industrial glazed deep grey which can bring a whiff of the factory to the garden. However, especially in the widely seen rope-edged pattern, this may bring an authentically gloomy touch to a Victorian scheme. Perhaps the most distinguished and versatile edging is made of narrow pieces of stone or plain tiles set edgeways and embedded in mortar.

These then are some of the materials used for paths and the principles of their use in gardens. All rules, however, must be tailored to the context. The photographs in this book have been chosen to show a wide range of paths in gardens of very different kinds in several different countries. Many of them show great subtlety and ingenuity in their use of materials and many confidently – and successfully – fly in the face of some of the principles I have described. In the end, it is the garden owner who, understanding intimately the changing face of his or her own garden in different seasons, is best placed to decide.

GRASS

10. *Spires of white* Galtonia candicans *rising behind an edging of catmint* (Nepeta × faassenii) *follow the lines of a cruciform arrangement of grass paths in this beautifully planned small garden.*

28

11. *Richly planted borders in a small enclosed garden contrast with the
strip of turf that separates them. The entrance to the path is given
emphasis by a pair of sentinel clipped yews* (Taxus baccata).

12. (left) *In this country setting a path is traced by a close-cut swathe across a meadow of tall grass displaying its swaying seedheads.*

29

13. (above) *A path ambles across pasture and curves out of sight – luring the visitor on to some unknown destination.*

14. *A more formal version of a path across grass in which an avenue of slender trees is planted in the longer grass and an elegant bench provides an unassertive eyecatcher.*

15. *A virtuoso arrangement of paths in the grand manner. In this formal garden grass paths are part of a restrained symphony of greens, making subtle contrast with the hedges of yew* (Taxus baccata) *and of hornbeam* (Carpinus betulus).

16. *Fallen rose petals scattered on a well-kept*
turf path leading through a romantic rose arbour
to the focal point of a chinoiserie bench.

33

17. *A straight close-cut path brings gentle formality to the edge of parkland where the pale seed-heads of the tall grass reach upwards.*

18. *A straight path is given emphasis by avenue-like clumps of daffodils and alignment on an opening in a hedge. Such sketchy visual definition of a path has subtle charm.*

34

21. *Small pieces of stone neatly laid on their edges swirl like a stream about informally planted beds, suiting perfectly the wild woodland setting.*

38

22. *Steps and a sinuously winding path merge in this American garden with a pronounced Japanese atmosphere. The natural stone shapes and gravel path, veiled by a fall of autumn leaves, blend artifice and nature.*

23. *Apart from the casually placed slabs of natural slate this garden seems like nature untouched. Such paths are especially appropriate in a woodland garden.*

24. *York stone flags treated informally can be very attractive. This path
is laid in an irregular patchwork, separated by tufts of aromatic
chamomile* (Chamaemelum nobile).

25. *Blue lias stone is very hard and difficult to cut. Here its rough surface makes a handsomely rustic – if slightly perilous – path skirting an exuberant mixed border.*

26. A slender row of hexagonal cement slabs, winding its way across the turf, makes a striking and appropriate path among the heathers and azaleas of this woodland garden.

42

27. Although irregular in shape, the stones have been fitted together very tightly, giving a slightly formal character that harmonizes well with the symmetry of the raised borders with their repeated plantings of conifers.

*28. A beautifully designed path merging
harmoniously with steps that sweep smoothly
up a gentle slope.*

44

29. *A well-planned formal gravel path separating a lawn from a deep herbaceous border whose plants spill over on to the gravel.*

30. (above) *A stately gravel walk, gently cambered to shed rain quickly, leads down an avenue of holm oaks* (Quercus ilex).

31. (left) *A path of speckled chippings threads its way through lavishly planted informal borders. The jungle-like atmosphere is clearly emphasized here.*

46

32. *This well-made cambered path of sandy gravel is given immense character by its deep edging of box* (Buxus sempervirens) *clipped into billowing mounds and occasionally pierced by ferns.*

33. *An edging of pale granite setts defines this gravel path and provides relief to the sombre grey of the chippings.*

34. (right) *An irregular mixture of square yard-tiles and terracotta paviours give this path unusual character.*

48

35. (above) *Old yard-tiles, forming a strikingly textured path between fresh green hedges of box* (Buxus sempervirens), *are arranged in concentric circles round a central pot of the perennial wallflower* Erysimum *'Bowles' Mauve'.*

 OOD

36. *In this bamboo garden the wide paths are
made of sections of bamboo laid cross-wise.*

37. *Autumn leaves lie scattered on 'stepping stones' of sections of timber half embedded in the soil. Although dangerously slippery when wet, such simple paths are very effective in a woodland setting.*

38. *In this rather more formal woodland garden a noble path of wood
sections makes a handsome foil for massed plantings of Candelabra
primulas* (Primula pulverulenta).

39. *Densely planted wild flowers – heartsease, foxgloves, cowslips – all
but obliterate this little path of small sections of wood.*

53

40. *Fallen foliage gives an ephemeral autumnal surface to this woodland path as it winds its way through long grass to a handsome fountain.*

$\mathcal{B}$RICK

41. *In these profusely planted borders reds and purples predominate
and find a visual echo in the brick path which is laid in a repeating
pattern of calm formality.*

55

42. A 'cottage-style' path of old brick contrasts with the formal
box-edged compartments of a parterre planted with blocks of fuchsias
(Fuchsia magellanica 'Variegata' and F. 'Tom Thumb').

43. *The versatility of brick is shown well in this parterre-like*
formal garden. At the centre of a cruciform arrangement of paths
bricks are arranged in concentric courses round a pot with ornamental
topiary of box (Buxus sempervirens).

44. (left) *A roughly laid narrow path of bricks provides an unassuming and practical walk between the beds of this ornamental kitchen garden.*

45. (right) *In this formal* jardin potager *an effective pattern of two kinds of brick goes well with the topiary of box* (Buxus sempervirens), *standard gooseberry bushes and 'Iceberg' roses.*

46. (above) *A beautifully laid path of bricks in basket-weave pattern makes a harmonious entrance through this intimate garden.*
47. (right) *An intricate design of brick is slightly raised and edged with rows of brick at a slightly lower level.*

48. *Here irregularly coursed brick shows a decorative unevenness which contrasts effectively with the fine parterre and the imposing topiary entrance and ornamental pool beyond.*

60

49. *The symmetry of the façade of this elegant*
clapboard house is emphasized by a central path
of brick with raised edges and repeated plantings
of dahlias, roses and oriental poppies.

50. *In this formal town garden enclosed by brick walls, brick is used in many different ways. Paths are laid in a lively pattern and edged with rows of bricks laid sideways.*

SOURCES

Some UK Addresses

Countryside
ECC Building Products Ltd
Holland Ward
Derby
DE6 3ET
Telephone: (0335) 370600

Creation Landscapes
23 Hillcrest Parade
The Mount
Coulsdon
Surrey
CR3 2PS
Telephone: (081) 668 2917

Some US Addresses

Florentine Craftsmen
46-24 28th Street
Long Island City, NY 11101
Telephone: (718) 937-7632

International Terracotta Inc.
690 North Robertson Boulevard
Los Angeles, CA 90069-5088
Telephone: (213) 657-3752

Lynch, Kenneth & Sons, Inc.
PO Box 488
Wilton CT 06897-0488
Telephone: (203) 762-8363

Moultrie Manufacturing Co.
PO Drawer 1179
Moultrie, GA 31776 1179
Telephone: (800) 841-86741
in Georgia (912) 985-1312

Smith and Hawken
25 Corte Madera
Mill Valley, CA 94941
Telephone: (415) 383-4415

Southern Statuary and Stone
3401 Fifth Avenue South
Birmingham, AL 35222
Telephone: (205) 322-0379

PICTURE   CREDITS

The Publisher thanks the following photographers and
organizations for their kind permission to reproduce photographs
in this book.
Owners and designers of gardens are credited where known.
Photographers appear in bold type.

Title page. **Andrew Lawson**; Constantine, Falmouth, Cornwall
page 6. **Andrew Lawson**; Wootton Place, Woodstock, Oxfordshire
Picture No 1 **Andrew Lawson**; Woodbine Cottage, Hampton Bishop, Hereford
Picture No 2 **Derek Fell**; private garden, USA
Picture No 3 **Patrick Taylor**; The Garden House, Buckland Monachorum, Devon
Picture No 4 **Patrick Taylor**; Dumbarton Oaks, Washington DC, USA
Picture No 5 **Eric Crichton**; The National Trust, Tintinhull, Somerset
Picture No 6 **Eric Crichton**; Paul Hobhouse, Hapsden House, Somerset
Picture No 7 **Derek Fell**; Seattle Arboretum, Washington, USA
Picture No 8 **Eric Crichton**; Mrs H. Astor, Folly Farm, Berkshire
Picture No 9 **Eric Crichton**; Mrs M. Fuller, The Crossing House, Cambridgeshire
Picture No 10 **Jerry Harpur**; Kellie Castle, Tayside, Scotland
Picture No 11 **Patrick Taylor**; Walenburg, The Netherlands
Picture No 12 **Jerry Harpur**; Mrs Mirabel Osler, Ludlow, Shropshire
Picture No 13 **Andrew Lawson**; private garden, Oxfordshire
Picture No 14 **Andrew Lawson**; private garden, Oxfordshire
Picture No 15 **Patrick Taylor**; Walenburg, The Netherlands
Picture No 16 **Georges Lévêque**; Mark Rumary (garden architect), Westley Waterless,
Suffolk
Picture No 17 **Georges Lévêque**; private garden, Mont Saint André, Belgium
Picture No 18 **Eric Crichton**; Mrs R. R. Merton, The Rectory, Burghfield, Berkshire
Picture No 19 **Eric Crichton**; Mrs R. R. Merton, The Rectory, Burghfield, Berkshire
Picture No 20 **Jerry Harpur**; Mrs S. Spencer, York Gate, Leeds, Yorkshire
Picture No 21 **Andrew Lawson**; Nine Acres Close, Charlbury, Oxfordshire
Picture No 22 **Derek Fell**; Swiss Pines Garden, Pennsylvania, USA